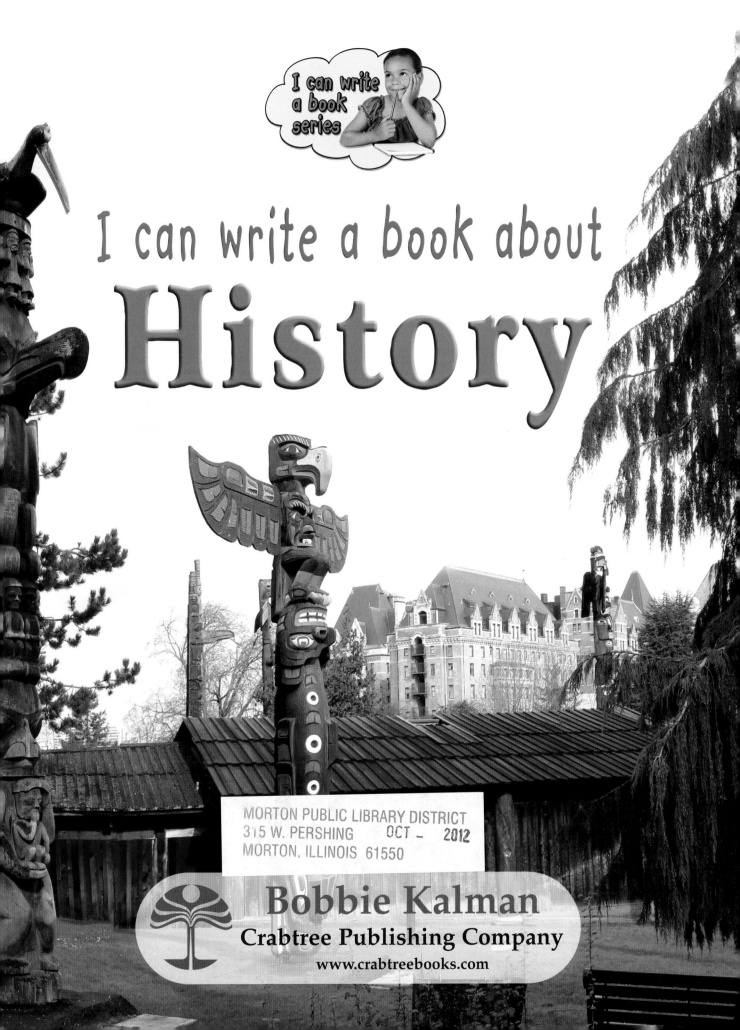

I can write a book series

I can write a book about
History

Bobbie Kalman
Crabtree Publishing Company
www.crabtreebooks.com

Created by Bobbie Kalman

Dedicated by Samantha and Bobbie
To "pioneer girl" Kiera Wilson Grant,
who loves being a part of history

Author and Editor-in-Chief
Bobbie Kalman

Editors
Kathy Middleton
Crystal Sikkens

Photo research
Bobbie Kalman

Design
Bobbie Kalman
Katherine Berti
Samantha Crabtree
(logo and cover)

Prepress technician
Katherine Berti

Print and production coordinator
Katherine Berti

Illustrations
Barbara Bedell: front cover (candlesticks and doll), back cover (top right, center right, and center left), p. 3, 4 (candlesticks and doll), 8 (all except top right), 9 (all except map), 10 (top right and bottom left), 11 (all except top, cowgirl, and tipi), 12 (all except cowboys), 13 (all except cabinetmaker and wheelwright), 15 (bottom right), 17 (bottom left), 19 (bottom), 20 (top right), 21 (top insets, all except purse), 23 (center left and bottom left), 26 (bottom left), 27 (left), 30 (top right inset and bottom right inset)
Halina Below-Spada: p. 27 (top right)
Antoinette "Cookie" Bortolon: front cover (quill pen and coal iron), p. 4 (quill pen)
Bonna Rouse: p. 8 (top right), 9 (map), 10 (bottom right), 11 (cowgirl and tipi), 12 (cowboys), 13 (cabinetmaker and wheelwright), 21 (bottom right insets)
Margaret Amy Salter: p. 21 (top inset, purse)

Photographs
Adobe/Image Club: p. 21 (bottom left inset)
Bobbie Kalman: front cover (barrels), back cover (inset), p. 5 (top left inset), 15 (top right), 26 (bottom right), 28 (bottom left inset)
Shutterstock: cover, logo, title page, p. 4 (boy, book, coffee mill, scroll), 5 (top book and bottom), 14, 15 (top left and bottom left), 16 (top), 17 (top right and bottom right), 18, 19 (top), 20 (bottom), 21 (books, letter M, and letter W), 22, 23 (top left and right), 24, 25, 26 (top right and center right), 27 (bottom), 28 (top right and bottom parchment), 29, 30 (bottom left inset), 31 (bottom left); Everett Collection: p. 13 (top), 17 (center left); Matt McClain: p. 16 (bottom); Jim Parkin: p. 17 (top left); Jeff Schultes: cover (book inset), p. 4 (book inset)
Thinkstock: Photos.com: p. 11 (top)
Wikimedia Commons: Andrew Dunn (zoetrope): p. 20; John Griffith (cooperage): p. 27 (computer inset)

Library and Archives Canada Cataloguing in Publication

Kalman, Bobbie
I can write a book about history / Bobbie Kalman.

(I can write a book series)
Includes index.
Issued also in electronic format.
ISBN 978-0-7787-7990-2 (bound).--ISBN 978-0-7787-7999-5 (pbk.)

1. Historiography--Juvenile literature. 2. Composition (Language arts)--Juvenile literature. 3. English language--Composition and exercises--Juvenile literature. 4. Book design--Juvenile literature.
I. Title. II. Series: Kalman, Bobbie. I can write a book.

D13.K25 2012   j907.2   C2012-901609-8

Library of Congress Cataloging-in-Publication Data

Kalman, Bobbie.
I can write a book about history / Bobbie Kalman.
p. cm. -- (I can write a book series)
Includes index.
ISBN 978-0-7787-7990-2 (reinforced library binding : alk. paper) -- ISBN 978-0-7787-7999-5 (pbk. : alk. paper) -- ISBN 978-1-4271-7881-7 (electronic pdf) -- ISBN 978-1-4271-7996-8 (electronic html)
1. Historiography--Juvenile literature. 2. Authorship--Juvenile literature. 3. Books--Juvenile literature. I. Title.

D13.K25 2012
808.06'69--dc23

2012008967

Crabtree Publishing Company

www.crabtreebooks.com   1-800-387-7650

Printed in Canada/042012/KR20120316

Published in Canada
Crabtree Publishing
616 Welland Ave.
St. Catharines, Ontario
L2M 5V6

Published in the United States
Crabtree Publishing
PMB 59051
350 Fifth Avenue, 59th Floor
New York, New York 10118

Published in the United Kingdom
Crabtree Publishing
Maritime House
Basin Road North, Hove
BN41 1WR

Published in Australia
Crabtree Publishing
3 Charles Street
Coburg North
VIC 3058

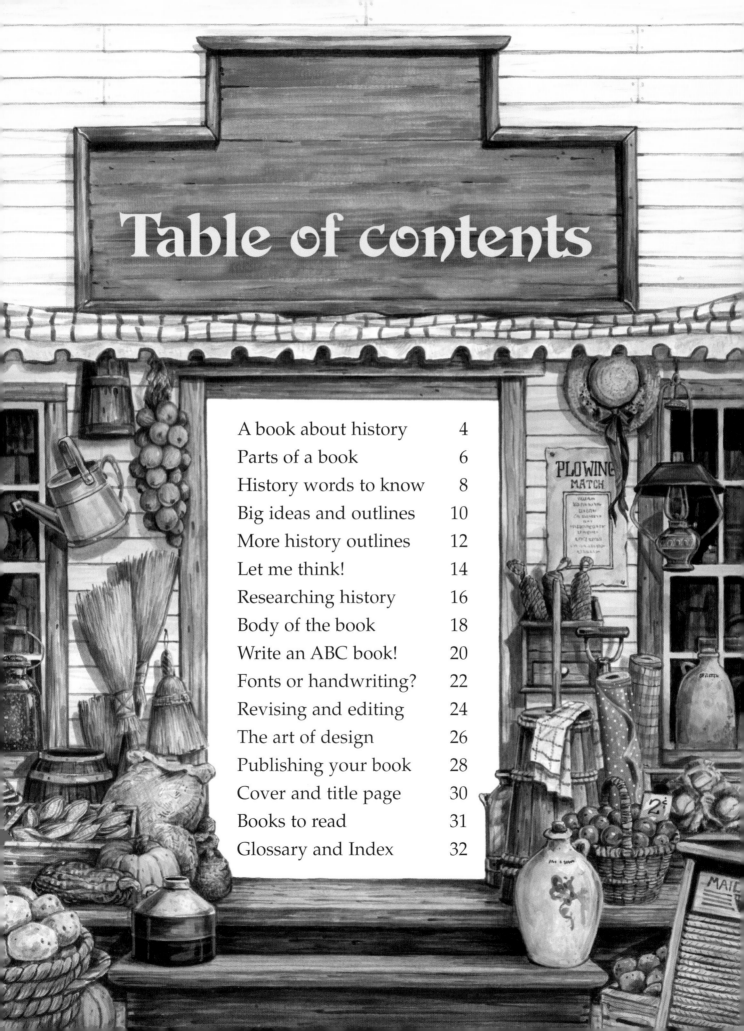

Table of contents

A book about history

History is a record of past events. Some stories from the past were passed down from grandparents to grandchildren. Other historic events are experienced by visiting historic communities such as **pioneer villages** and **colonial towns**. Most of history is written in **non-fiction** books. A **fiction** book is not a true story, but a non-fiction book contains stories about real people or facts about animals, habitats, countries, culture, and many other subjects. This non-fiction book teaches how to write and **publish** a non-fiction book about history. To publish is to share the final copy of a book with others.

When you write about a subject you like, you will have fun. The more you learn about that subject, the more you will want to learn. Publishing your book will make you feel proud!

A historic community
by Me

Bobbie's promise

I am an **author** of many children's books. The first books I wrote were about history. To write these books, I immersed myself and my family in the past. I dressed in costumes and "became" a character in whatever I was writing about. This picture shows me and my daughter, Samantha, who spent much of her time "living" history with me. We traveled to historic places, took part in activities, and had photographs taken of ourselves for the books. Everything I saw, read, and experienced made me feel excited about writing books, and I couldn't wait to share the information and excitement with my readers. You will feel the same when you write and publish your book about history. I promise!

Learning and teaching

When you write a book, you learn a lot about a subject. The more you learn, the more you will want to know. When you discover how people lived in the past, you also learn about your life right now. Writing a book is a great way to share your knowledge! When others read your book, they will be learning from you. Besides being an author, you will be a teacher, too.

What history topic will you write about?

Parts of a book

Does your teacher ask you to write reports? Writing a non-fiction book is like writing a report, but there are more parts and pages to a book. A book's pages are held together by a **cover**. A cover is the outside of the book. It is the first thing that people see. When people see an interesting cover, they want to read the book. The cover shown here is the cover of this book. Your cover will be different (see page 30). What will you put on the cover of your book about history?

*The back cover of the book may give you information about the author, **publisher**, price, and other books written by the author.*

*The **spine** of the book has the title, author, and publisher's name. It helps you find a book on a bookshelf.*

The front cover of the book contains the title of the book and the name of the author. It catches your attention with an interesting title or a great picture or pictures.

The title page

The first page inside the cover is the **title page**. The picture on the right shows the title page of this book. What information does it give you?

Copyright page

The second page in this book is the **copyright** page. Copyright means that people cannot copy all or parts of the book without the author's or publisher's permission. What else does it tell you? Turn to the copyright page in this book and find the following information:

- the names of the people who helped create this book
- the addresses of the publisher
- the **dedication** of the book, or the words used to honor someone by placing his or her name in the book
- the **cataloging information**, a section of the page that tells the book's title, the name of the author, the year the book was published, and the type of book it is

Contents, glossary, index

The **table of contents** gives the names of the **chapters**, or sections, in the book and the page numbers on which they begin. The **glossary** is a small dictionary that explains special words used in the book. The **index** is an alphabetical list of the topics in the book with page numbers telling where those topics are covered.

I can write a book about **History**

Bobbie Kalman
Crabtree Publishing Company
www.crabtreebooks.com

The page above shows the title page, and the page below shows the table of contents of this book.

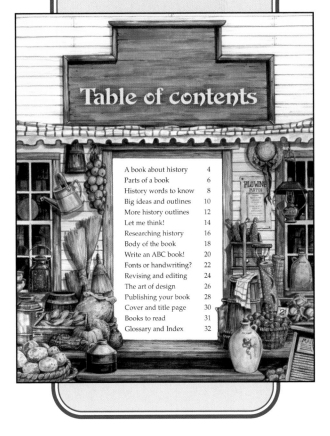

Table of contents

History words to know

These two pages introduce you to some important words about history. They give you information that will help you write your book. Important words are usually contained in a glossary at the end of a book. For your own book, you can do a picture dictionary with definitions underneath, like these examples, or a glossary without pictures, or both. (See page 29 to find out how to write your glossary.)

apprentice

An **apothecary** prepares and sells medicine. An **apprentice** learns a job by working with a skilled person, like an apothecary.

A **blacksmith** is a worker who shapes iron into objects such as farm tools, cooking pots, and horseshoes.

A **cabinetmaker** is a maker of good-quality furniture.

A **colony** is a place ruled by a faraway country. People who lived in a colony were called **colonists**. **Colonial** describes things, such as homes or towns, which were part of the colonies. The colonial period in the United States lasted from the 1600s to 1776, when the country became **independent**, or free, from England.

A **cooper** makes barrels and buckets.

A **craftsperson** is a skilled worker who makes objects by hand. A **farrier** trims the hooves of horses and puts shoes on them.

A **general store** sells items, such as food, cloth, clothing, tools, and dishes. The store owner is called a **merchant**.

A **gristmill** is a building in which grains such as wheat and corn are ground into flour. The **miller** is the person who runs the mill.

*A **log house** is a home built from huge logs.*

Native peoples were the first peoples to live in **North America**. There were many native **nations**, or groups. They lived in different areas, spoke different languages, and had different ways of life.

This map of North America shows where some native nations lived.

*An **outbuilding** is a small building, such as this chicken coop, which is not part of the main house.*

*A **pioneer** or **settler** is a person who moves into a new area to make a home where few others live.*

*A **village** is a small community. Pioneer villages had a general store, a gristmill, and craftspeople.*

Other words

A **ranch** is a large farm where cattle or sheep are raised (see page 12).

A **slave** is a person who is forced to work without pay.

Victorian is the period in history from 1837 to 1901, when Queen Victoria ruled. During this time, some people built fancy homes and lived more comfortable lives.

Big ideas and outlines

When you write a book about history, there are several **big ideas**, or important topics, to explore. The next four pages show some of these. They will help you write your book. What history topics are you studying at school? Have you ever visited a historic community such as a pioneer village or a colonial town? What interested you the most during your visit? Have you dressed in a historic costume for a parade or historic celebration? What kind of activities could you include in your book? You could find some pioneer recipes, do an ABC book, or make up a quiz about life in a historic community.

Historic communities

Today, there are many historic communities in which people **reenact** life long ago. By writing a book on history, you will also be able to show what life was like then. Pages 11–13 give you some outlines that will help you write your own history book.

*In colonial and pioneer times, people traveled long distances in **stagecoaches**. After a long day on the road, stagecoaches stopped at inns, where people could get a meal and stay overnight.*

In early homes, meals were cooked over a fire in a huge fireplace. The fireplace also heated the home.

*Many people in North America moved west to start new lives there. **Boomtowns**, or towns that grew quickly, offered jobs to workers of all kinds.*

Community outline

These topics can be used for a book about a colonial, pioneer, or western community, or about Victorian life.

• What is a historic community?
• Who were the people?
• Different homes
• The kitchen
• The craftspeople
• The gristmill
• General store
• Special shops
• Travel on water and land
• Education and schools
• Clothing styles
• Work and play

life in a Victorian home

children's games

colonial craftspeople

cowgirl on ranch

raising sheep to make wool clothing

Native communities

Native people lived throughout North America. See the map on page 9 to see where some native nations lived.

• Native nations coast to coast
• Native homes
• Native clothing
• Foods from the land
• Children's lives
• Travel on land and water
• Life in a longhouse village
• Nations of the Great Lakes
• Nations of the Plains
• Nations of the Southwest
• Nations of the Northwest Coast
• The nations of the Far North

teaching children

Plains nation tipi

Inuit of the Far North

totem pole of a Northwest Coast nation

Eastern Great Lakes

More history outlines

Home outline

Home is where people live. Whether you are writing about a colonial home, a pioneer home, a ranch, or a Victorian home, you can use some of these topics or add your own.

- Homes made of logs
- Homemade furniture
- Later homes
- Who built the homes?
- The important kitchen
- The fireplace
- The outbuildings
- Homes for animals
- Bed chambers
- Vegetable gardens
- Work parties
- Decorating the home
- Servants in the home

Early colonial and pioneer homes were just one room with a fireplace.

*The pioneers had work parties called **bees**. They built barns or made quilts together and then celebrated with a meal, dancing, and games.*

cowboys

Many cattle ranches, shown right, were built in the West. Cowboys looked after the cattle and horses.

12

A one-room school

In some pioneer communities, children attended a one-room school. Students of all ages studied together in the same classroom and were taught by one teacher.

- The schoolhouse
- The teacher
- Reading, writing, and arithmetic
- School supplies
- Getting to school
- Classroom games
- Recess games
- Special days
- The school garden

Craftspeople outline

There were few machines in the 18th and 19th centuries. Craftspeople made the items that people needed.

- Learning their crafts
- The cooper
- The blacksmith and farrier
- Other metalworkers
- The boot maker
- The harness maker
- The cabinetmaker
- The wheelwright
- Housewrights

blacksmith

farrier

harness maker

wheelwright

housewrights (house builders)

cooper

cabinetmaker

Let me think!

To begin writing your book, you first need to decide what you want to write about. Picking topics that interest you will make writing your book more fun. You can use a "writer's notebook" to record your ideas, thoughts, and information that you have learned. The questions below will help you decide which history topics are right for you.

Will I write my book on a computer or by hand?

Questions to ask myself

- Do I want to write about a colonial, pioneer, western, or native community?
- Which historic community have I visited that I want to learn more about?
- What do I already know about life in that historic community?
- How will I make my book exciting for others to read?
- How will I collect all the information I need?
- How will I find pictures or artwork of historic places or objects?
- How will I present the information in my book? Could I write an ABC book?
- Will I work alone or with some other students in my class?

Prewriting

- There are many fascinating subjects in history! Choose ones that interest you and learn all about them.

- Make an outline of the topics you will be writing about. Your outline will become your table of contents.

Bobbie's team

Over the years, I have worked with writing teams, as shown above. My writing team helped me research, write, and make corrections on my books. While writing books about history, my team and I often visited historic communities dressed in costumes, so we could "feel" part of the past. Perhaps you could form a writing team and share the work you are doing on some historic books. You could write an ABC book together (see pages 20–21) and divide the letters so everyone has different topics, or follow some of the outlines on pages 11–13. Visiting a historic community will give you an excellent start!

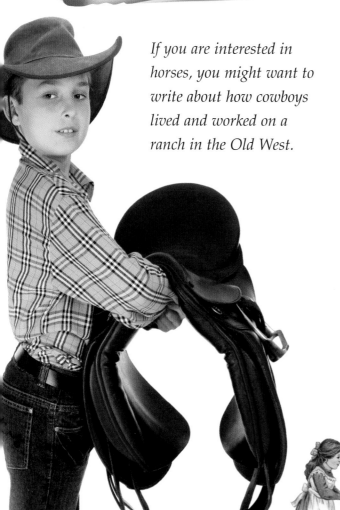

If you are interested in horses, you might want to write about how cowboys lived and worked on a ranch in the Old West.

Researching history

There is information about historic communities in this book, but you will need to **research**, or gather more information, to put into your book. Reading the books on page 31 is a good start. They may be in your school or public library. You can also find information in other books, encyclopedias, and on the Internet. There are great videos on historic places, as well! With your teacher's or parent's permission, you can do a **virtual tour** of a pioneer village or colonial town, such as Williamsburg. Take notes in your writer's notebook. Look for details that interest you and learn more about those things.

Watching videos of historic communities is almost like being there. Watch several videos from different communities and compare the clothing, homes, shops, and craftspeople you saw.

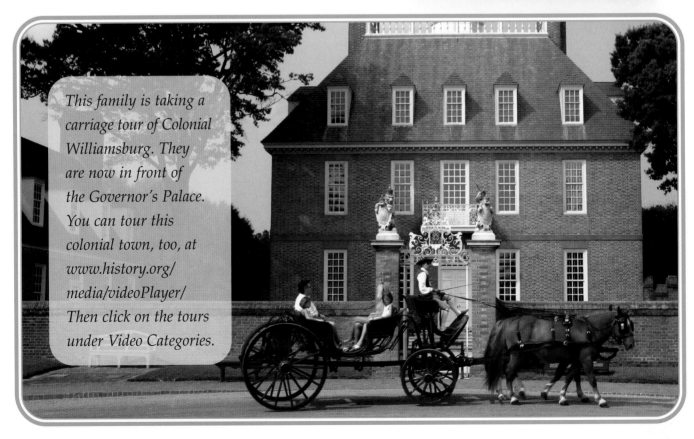

This family is taking a carriage tour of Colonial Williamsburg. They are now in front of the Governor's Palace. You can tour this colonial town, too, at www.history.org/ media/videoPlayer/ Then click on the tours under Video Categories.

These children did some laundry the pioneer way—without a washing machine! In the days of the pioneers, there were very few machines. Everything was done by hand.

Research help

- Use at least two research sources. Do not copy the information word for word. Write it in your own words.
- Read some novels about pioneer life, such as the Little House on the Prairie books by Laura Ingalls Wilder.
- Which machines do we use today for doing laundry, cooking, and keeping food fresh? Compare how these things were done in a historic community.

Ask your grandparents if any of your ancestors lived on a ranch and helped train horses like this young cowboy?

This woman is taking vegetables down to a **root cellar** to keep them cool and fresh. How is food kept fresh today?

Did your great-great-grandmother dress like these women? Would you like to dress like this? Why or why not?

Body of the book

Now that you have done some research on the topics in your outline, it is time to start writing the **body** of the book. The body of your book will contain the information you have learned and want to share with others.

Chapters, paragraphs, headings

An easy way to start writing your book is to divide it into small chapters called **spreads**. A spread is two pages that face each other. Each topic in your outline can be a spread. The **heading** tells the reader what topic is being covered. Most spreads have several paragraphs. A **subheading**, which is smaller than the chapter heading, tells what a paragraph is about. What is the heading of this spread? What are the subheadings?

In each book I write, I cover one main topic on each spread. When you write about a topic this way, your information, ideas, and pictures are much easier to organize. The spread above is from *A Visual Dictionary of a Pioneer Community* (see page 31).

Different writing styles

To make your book more exciting to read, try writing some sections in these text styles:

- **Informational** text gives information. Most of this book is written as informational text.
- **Instructional** text gives directions on how to do something. Instructional text can be found on **parchment** pages throughout this book, such as the one on the right. Try this writing style in your own book.
- **Narrative** text is written in story form. Write a story about a day: in a one-room school; working as an apprentice; or living as a slave in a colonial home.
- **Descriptive** text describes a place or thing using the senses of sight, smell, hearing, taste, and touch (or feel).

Imagine!

1. Imagine you are the slave boy or girl in the picture below and write a narrative about a day in your life. Talk about your family and the work you do each day.

2. Write descriptive text about your experience in this kitchen. What do you **see**? What sounds do you **hear**? How will the pie **smell** when it is baking? How will it **taste** when it is done? How does the firewood **feel** against your skin? What makes this kitchen seem warm and cozy?

Write an ABC book!

Alphabet books are fun to write. They allow you to be extra creative. You can write about one topic on each spread or choose more than one. The words in the book below are suggestions to get you started. You can find many of them on pages 8–13. Draw your own pictures using the pictures in this book as your guides.

zoetrope

History from A to Z

A is for apothecary, apprentice

B is for blacksmith, boot maker, boys, bees

C is for children, colonial, cooper, chores, clothing, craftsperson, cowboy

D is for dwelling, dress, dishes

E is for education, elder, east

F is for family, farrier, fireplace, food

G is for gristmill, general store, girls, games, gardens

H is for home, history, hunting, harness

I is for inn, iron, Inuit

J is for jobs, journal, journey, jump rope

K is for kitchen, kettle, knickers

L is for lathe, leatherworker, log house

M is for merchant, mill, miller, milliner

N is for native nations, north, nosegay

O is for outbuildings, one-room school

P is for pioneer, plank house, parties

Q is for questions, quilt, quill pen

R is for rag rug, reading, ranches

S is for settler, slave, south, saddle, slate

T is for trade, territory, travel, toys

U is for undergarments, utensils

V is for village, vegetables, Victorian

W is for West, wagon trains, women, wheelwright, wool

X is for Xmas

Y is for yard goods, yarn, your

Z is for zigzag fence, zoetrope

M is for milliner.

Milliners make hats, but colonial milliners did much more. They sold fashion items, such as hats, purses, gowns, cloaks, shoes, gloves, fans, masks, muffs, stockings, and jewelry.

Draw pictures and write about these items sold by the milliner.

purse

choker

stockings

hat

feathers

mask

neckerchief

muff

pockets

shoes

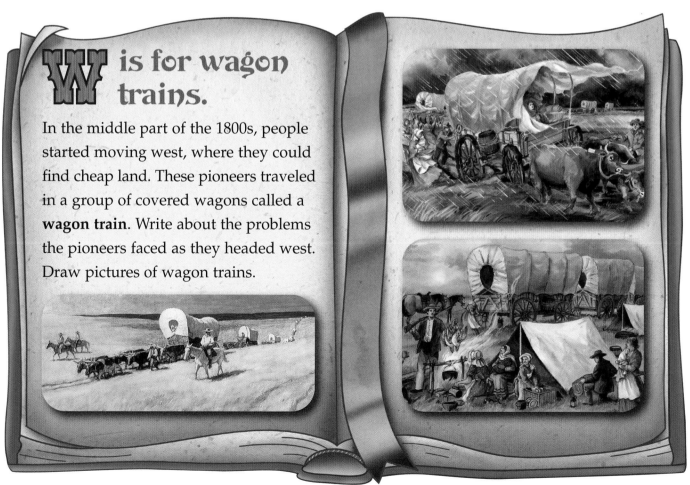

W is for wagon trains.

In the middle part of the 1800s, people started moving west, where they could find cheap land. These pioneers traveled in a group of covered wagons called a **wagon train**. Write about the problems the pioneers faced as they headed west. Draw pictures of wagon trains.

Fonts or handwriting?

There are different ways to write. If you are using a computer, you have many choices. If you are writing your book by hand, you can use colors and different ways of writing that look like the words on a computer.

Different fonts

A **font** is a style of type. Most of this book is written in a **plain text** font, but you will notice other kinds of fonts, as well. Words that are written in a **boldface**, or thick black, font are words that may be new to you. Sometimes they are explained on the page, and sometimes they are defined in the glossary. The headings and subheadings are in larger type. A different font is used to make them stand out from the rest of the text. Headings may also be in color. Choose colors that match the pictures on the pages.

What are captions?

The text that gives you information about a picture is called a **caption**. The captions in this book are written in *italics*. Letters in italics slant to the right and are smaller than plain text. **Fact boxes** bring attention to special information, ask questions, or give instructions. There are several fact boxes in this book. They are on parchment paper, such as the one above right.

Choosing fonts

- If you are writing your book on a computer, try using some different fonts.
- Choose a plain text font that is easy to read.
- Choose heading fonts that suit your subject.
- If you are writing your book by hand, use a thick pencil, pen, or marker to make words look like **boldface**.
- Write captions by *slanting* your words to look like an *italic* font.
- For headings, use markers or colored pencils.

Practice caption writing

Write captions for the pictures on this page.
Use your imagination!

Write a caption about what activities these girls might take part in at this pioneer village.

What dangers might the passengers in this sleigh face traveling in winter?

How did the pioneers work and have fun, too? What were work parties called? What are these women making?

Revising and editing

Once you have written your **draft**, or first try at writing your book, you should read it through from front to back. While reading, ask yourself these questions:

- How does my draft sound?
- Have I included all the information I wanted to include?
- Have I included my own observations or experiences with history?
- Have I used descriptive details using my senses?
- Do my captions give interesting information? Do they describe what is happening in the pictures?
- Do my sentences make sense?
- Did I use **comparisons**?
- Have I asked questions to make my readers think?
- How can I **revise**, or rewrite, my book to make it better?

Ask a parent or your teacher to give you ideas on how to organize and improve your work.

Share your draft

- After you have read your draft and made some changes, it is time to share it with others.
- Read your draft loudly and clearly at least twice. Ask your listeners to make notes on what they did not understand.
- Ask them which parts of your writing still needs to be revised.
- Ask the listeners what they liked or did not like about your draft.
- Listen to the **feedback** that your listeners give you about your writing.
- How did the comments of your listeners make you feel about your book?

Editing checklist

Editing is making sure your writing is clear and correct.

- Have you covered all the topics you intended to cover?
- Have you used new and interesting words?
- Do your subheadings reflect the information in your paragraphs?

Proofreading checklist

Proofreading is checking for errors such as spelling mistakes, capital letters, and **punctuation**.

- Are your sentences complete?
- Have you used the correct punctuation and capitals?
- Have you spelled names and other words correctly?

Don't worry about making mistakes! Every author rewrites his or her book many times.

*If you are not sure how to spell a word or whether you used the correct word, look it up in a dictionary. To find new and interesting words for your book, use a **thesaurus**. A thesaurus gives **synonyms** for words. A synonym is a word that means the same as another word.*

Questions help you

There are many questions in this book. How do questions help you?

- They help you review what you have written and think about what you still need to write.
- They help you think of better ways to write your book.
- Asking people questions helps you learn new information.

The art of design

Designing is planning how your book will look so that people will want to read it. Writing text in a certain way, such as in fact boxes, is part of design. Using different fonts and colors also makes the book more attractive to readers.

Take pictures while visiting a historic village or photograph pioneer projects you have made.

Artwork and photographs

The other very important part of design is placing different kinds of pictures in your book. Pictures attract readers and make them want to read more. You can draw and paint your own pictures or take photographs of historic sites. You can also download photos from the Internet (see page 27). Print these pictures and put them into your book. Look at the design of the spreads in this book to give you ideas about how to design your own book.

Draw some pictures for your book using the illustrations in this book as your guide.

These elementary school children made a rag rug for me as part of their pioneer studies. You can make a rag rug, too, by braiding three strips of cloth together and then sewing it into a round rug like this one. Take photos of the rug for your book.

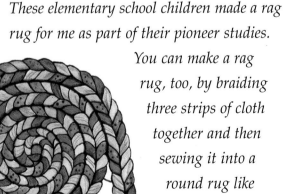

Draw diagrams

Draw and label diagrams that will help your readers understand your information. This diagram shows how a gristmill works.

*Water from a pond made the **waterwheel** turn, which turned the **gearwheels**. The gearwheels turned the **runner.** The runner ground the grain into flour as it turned.*

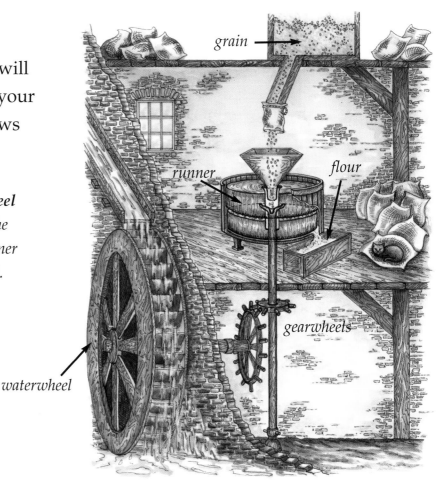

grain

Download pictures

Ask a parent or teacher to show you how to find and download pictures from the Internet. Do a search of the kinds of photographs or art you need. Many works of art and photographs can be downloaded for free. The picture inside the laptop below is free to use by anyone. When you download a picture, make sure you include the **source**, or where you obtained the picture. There are many historic pictures you can download.

*The photo on the right is of a **cooperage**, or where a cooper made and sold barrels. It is in Black Creek Pioneer Village. Just do a search of pioneer village or colonial town photos, and you will find many.*

Publishing your book

Publishing your book is the last step. Many schools place the books students have written in the library for other students to read. Does your library have a publishing program for students? If you did your book on the computer, you could make an eBook that many students could enjoy.

Important pages

Before you publish your book on the computer or by hand, you will need to complete all the parts of the book mentioned on pages 6 and 7: the copyright page; table of contents; the glossary; and index. Find these pages in this book.

You may need to ask a parent or teacher to help you finish designing your book on the computer.

Bobbie's reminder

The pages shown opposite are very important because they help your reader find and understand the information in your book. They also thank people who helped you edit, proofread, and design your book, as well as credit the sources of photographs and art. You can also include a **bibliography**, or a list of books and their authors, that you used for your research. Use the copyright page in this book as an example of how to write one for your book.

Copyright page

Your copyright page will include all the people who helped you with your book: your classmates, parents, teacher, and librarian. This page may also include a dedication. To whom will you dedicate your book?

Table of contents

Your table of contents is a list of the headings of all the spreads you wrote. Their page numbers are placed at the right or left of the headings. Your table of contents is a revised list of your outline. (See the table of contents in this book.)

Glossary

There is a picture dictionary on pages 8-9 in this book, but your glossary can just be words, like the glossary on page 32. Use a dictionary to define any words that you did not know or your readers may not know. Sort your glossary in alphabetical order.

Index

The index is a list of the names and topics that readers may look for in a book. It is in alphabetical order and gives the page numbers of where to find topics in your book. The index on page 32 will help you write your index.

After you have finished the inside of the book, print off or photocopy all your pages. Use the photocopies for your book and save the originals. That way, you can make more copies of your handwritten pages and art, if you need to publish additional books.

Cover and title page

There are different ways to present your book to your readers. In some schools, the teacher or librarian has ways of **binding**, or tying, the pages of books together so other students can read them without losing pages. One of the easiest ways to keep your book together is to photocopy all your pages and then slip each one into a binder with plastic sleeves. These binders often have plastic pockets on the front and back, as well. You can put your cover pictures into those. The spine will also have a thin plastic pocket for your title. On the right is a sample title page. Below is a front and back cover with a spine.

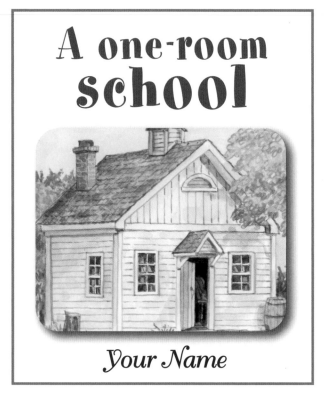

A one-room school

Your Name

title page

About the author
Write something about yourself and why you enjoyed writing this book.

A ONE-ROOM SCHOOL   YOUR NAME

A one-room school

Your Name

back cover   *spine*   *front cover*

Books to read

The books shown here were written by me, Bobbie Kalman. Find them in your library. They will help you write your book.

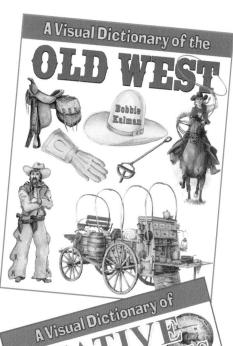

Further research

Learn more about history by reading other titles in these series:

- Historic Communities
- Colonial People
- Life in the Old West
- Native Nations of North America

Glossary

Note: Some boldfaced words are defined where they appear in the book.

comparison The act of determining the likenesses and differences in a situation, object, or event

descriptive A writing style that uses the five senses of sight, hearing, smell, taste, and touch

informational A writing style that gives information about something

instructional A writing style that gives instructions or directions on how to do something

narrative A writing style that tells something in story form

parchment Dried, thin animal skin, or paper that resembled it, on which people wrote a long time ago

publisher A person or company that is responsible for printing and distributing a written book

punctuation The use of marks, such as periods or commas, to make the meaning of a sentence clear

root cellar An underground or partly underground pit that was covered with earth and used to store vegetables

stagecoach A carriage pulled by horses

virtual tour A video tour of a place that can be watched on the Internet

Index